Paperback Quarterly

*"Journal of the
American Paperback Institute"*

CONTENTS

The Pecan Valley Press
Brownwood, Texas

PAPERBACK QUARTERLY features articles and notes dealing with every type (mystery, detective, science fiction, western, adventure, etc.) and with every aspect of new, old and rare paperbacks.

Emphasis is placed on the historical research of paperbacks, their authors, illustrators, publishers and distributors; but the editors also invite contributions of bibliographical interest. In short, the only criterion for the editor's consideration is that the subject matter pertain to paperbacks.

PQ pays ½¢ per word (600-4,000 words) for articles and notes. Payment on acceptance.

PQ is published in Spring, Summer, Fall and Winter of each year with a subscription rate of $6.00 per year or individual copies for $2.00 each. Institutional and library subscriptions are $8.00. Overseas rate is $12.00.

All back issues are out of print.

All correspondence, articles, notes, queries, ads and subscriptions should be sent to 1710 Vincent Street, Brownwood, Texas 76801. (915) 643-1182.

Billy C. Lee...................Editor & Publisher
Charlotte Laughlin............Contributing Editor
Bill Crider...................Contributing Editor
Thomas Bonn...................Contributing Editor
Shawn Loudermilk..............Editor
Shelly Campbell...............Editor
Martin E. Gottschalk..........Printer & Technical Advisor
Peter Manesis.................Cover Logo Designer

Copyright © 1979 by Billy C. Lee
All Rights Reserved
Printed in the United States of America

Letters from Our Readers

Dear Billy,

If no one else is going to say it, I will: the
Summer issue was superb, a nice mixture of interviews
and articles. Too bad more readers aren't writing,
however. Also too bad the first leter had such a
snotty tone. Oh well. I've been telling some
paperback artists (e.g., McGinnis, Bama, Abbett)
about your journal; I hope they write.

M.C. Hill's checklist of Dell 10¢ books was good
to see; #27's cover was done by Barye Phillips, by
the way. And the series did begin and end in 1951;
the idea was Don Ward's, after prompting by Lloyd
Smith of Western Printing & Lithographing for
employees to come up with new ideas for paperback
formats. One of the people who worked on the 10¢
line was James Gunn (now a noted author); he
suggested the cover, wrote the blurb, and wrote the
anonymous introduction for the only s-f title, #36.
Several of the books were filmed; RAIN several times,
of course (the story of
Sadie Thompson),
BEACHCOMBER (with Charles
Laughton); DEATH WALKS
MARBLE HALLS as QUIET
PLEASE, MURDER, 1942),
PAL JOEY, of course, and
YOU'LL NEVER SEE ME
AGAIN, recently as a TV-
movie, I think. These
in addition to the ones
Hill mentions.

I have been sniffing my
Monarch books, with no
results.   Best,

Bill Lyles

3

Dear Mr. Lee,

I enjoyed Howard Waterhouse's article on Avon's
MURDER MYSTERY MONTHLY very much, and the photos
of the covers demonstrated a cover art technique
that some collectors may not be aware of. The cover
illo for THE SHIP OF ISHTAR (#34, 1945), shown on
page 33 [PQ, Winter 1978], is a repainting of the
May 10, 1930 ARGOSY illustrating the first install-
ment of Kenneth Perkins's serial, VOODOO'D. This
ARGOSY cover painting has been changed only by
changing the original dark coat, white collar, and
red tie to Avon's striped pajama top. Another
example of repainting pulp covers is the covers is
the cover to Avon #122, R. Austin Freeman's THE
UNCONSCIOUS WITNESS (1947). This is a repainting
of the cover illo of PRIVATE DETECTIVE STORIES,
October 1944. In this one, a moustache is added
to the gun-wielding hero, and an anachronistic
radio microphone is deleted. Was this a common
practice for Avon?

Also a footnote to the movie editions article
[PQ,Spring 1979] -- I have two interesting
Century Publications movie paperbacks. The first
is digest sized, Century Mystery #37, SINGAPORE
(1947) by William G. Bogart. A montage of illustrations is on the front cover, and on the back
are three photos from the film. 17 stills are
inside, on the same stock as the text. Another
(Century Movie Book #68, 1947) is A DOUBLE LIFE,
as SINGAPORE, but is true paperback size rather
than digest.

I enjoy your magazine very much, particularly
the cover repros (the color shots are wonderful--
please continue this), and the articles on pb's of
the 40's and early 50's. For this reason I did
not much care for the Borgo Press article, which
read more like a promotional piece. Please keep
up the overviews on older series and interviews
with writers -- these are fascinating.

Best wishes,
Chet Williamson

Dear Billy,

This is in response to Bill Lyles's letter in PQ, Vol. 2, No. 2, concerning Western's place among paperback manufacturers. The issue I originally raised in my Vol. 2, No. 1 letter is that Western Publishing is not recognized as having "produced the most paperbacks from 1939 to 1976" as stated in Bill Lyles's original letter in Vol. 1, No. 3. My observation, not quoted completely in Bill's last letter, was "This statement as it stands could be quite misleading, as Wester, to the best of my knowledge, ranks as the third leading producer of paperback books." I chose the words in this observation carefully, hoping not to give umbrage, but expressing an observation which, I believe, is shared by most people in the publishing industry.

Over the last 18 years I have frequently discussed paperback manufacturing with publishing production people and manufacturing representatives to paperback publishers. On these occasions industry people, much more knowledgeable than I, have described W.F. Hall as the "largest" manufacturer (titles and quantity) of rack-size paperback books, with Arcata Graphics a fairly close second. This ranking of size, I believe, could be described as "common knowledge."

Before mailing my original letter on this subject, I sent a draft to Robert O'Connor of the W.F. Hall Company and asked him to check the facts. Mr. O'Connor has been for many years Hall's New York representative to paperback publishers; his father, Harry O'Connor, was the representative before him. Together with son and brother, Charles, this family goes back to the early days of paperback book manufacturing. Robert O'Connor found nothing inaccurate in the letter.

5

Bill Lyles rests Western's production on the 10,000 entries of the Western card files in the Library of Congress. As he stated, these note work not only for Dell but also for many other paperback publishers. (The fact that Avon, Ballantine, etc. have dealings with Western does not surprise me. Few, if any, paperback publishers sign exclusive manufacturing contracts with a printer. Even Dell, which perhaps comes the closest of any mass market publisher today to having an exclusive arrangement, as they have in the past, manufactures with other concerns.)

Bill has not actually described these 10,000 entries. Do they include Dell? Are they for new publications, or do they cover reprintings and reissues of the same publication?

Further, when considering "most paperbacks" are we dealing with total number of copies or titles, mass market and trade paperback, or just mass market? My own sweeping statement intended to define Hall, Arcata, and Western as ranking 1,2,3 in production of both titles and copies of mass market paperbacks only.

No one knows with any certainty how many new and new reprints have been published since 1939. Yet when one considers some of the following figures, the "10,000" figure shrinks considerably and leaves the position of Western as having "produced the most paperbacks' in my mind open for further consideration.

Pocket Books recently estimated publishing 12-15M titles since 1939. NAL estimates its output at about half that number. These are only two of how many mass market publishers that have issued books since 1939?

The current issue of Paperbound Books in Print

LISTS 167,340 different titles in print. Somewhere between 15-20% of these are mass market paperbacks. The overall annual publication rate of new mass market books and new mass market editions has been roughly 1,900 titles for each of the last two years.

These figures alone indicate to me that Bill's 10,000 entries, spread over 35 years or so, are subject to question if they are the sole support for his claim that Western "produced the most paperbacks."

This letter in no way intends to belittle Western's contribution to mass market paperback publishing. Western is, in my mind, the most important of the three leading book manufacturers because of its past association with Pocket Books, through the Golden Press, and because for almost for almost twenty years it was 2/3s of Dell Books. My original heavy-handed attempt was to simple question his statement and, more important, take the opportunity to outline the major steps in the manufacture of softcover books. It was not in any way intended to put Bill Lyles "in his place." Bill is doing all collectors and amateur publishing historians (and I include myself in their number) a great service by researching in LC archives and elsewhere this unique printing and publishing operation. I admire his industry and always appreciate the publication of his discoveries.

I hope that Bill continues to issue relevant information about Dell and Western and, further, that he will allow us to question from time to time statements that do not appear accurate.

Sincerely,
Thomas Bonn

Dear Billy,
Thanks to Tom Bonn for sending his response to my response to his initial letter before publication in PQ. It doesn't matter to me who's number 1 -- that's a number I find exciting only on a paperback. And I'm not about to describe the card file of Western at the Library of Congress: I last looked at it in March (only for the Dell information), and I'm now 400 miles away from Washington, D.C. and doubt if I'll return in the next decade. I hope I won't be held to an amount (10,000) that I estimated quickly. And I hope someone (besides me) makes use of the L.C. files. That's it, finis, my last word. 'Bye.

Best,
Bill Lyles

Dear Billy,
     Just a brief note to keep you abreast of what's happening in my part of the world. Enclosed you will find a copy of a questionnaire which Piet Schreuders and I have combined to compose and send to cover artists we have identified. Mention of the questionnaire in the next PQ and the fact that I am anxious to get in touch with cover artists would be greatly appreciated.
     This is my last month for awhile here at Cortland. I recently recieved approval for 5 months leave so that I can go off and write the history and gather together illustrations.
     Last week I received some very exciting news that the chapter on paperback book collecting that I drafted almost a year ago will be published next month by Bowker in something called Collectable Books: Some New Paths. The chapter I wrote has been ex- cerpted by the Washington Post and is to appear in the October 7th issue of their review Book World, which is to be devoted to paperback publishing. This came as a complete surprise and a very pleasant one at that. ....
     ....I hope things for you are grounding into shape. Regards to Charlotte.
                              Sincerely,
                              Tom Bonn

PAPERBACK

WRITERS

----------BILL CRIDER

In the past I've devoted this space to writers of paperback originals, but Mickey Spillane is a special case. He's the man whose work sold so well in reprints that it in a way paved the road for the original paperback novel. He had sold over 40 million of his Mike Hammer books in paper by the early 60s.

I discovered Spillane in an episode that sounds like a "Happy Days" rerun, but it's true. It was in homeroom in some now-forgotten year of high school. John Black, who sat in front of me turned around after the roll check and said, "Read this! You'll never believe it!" Then he handed me a copy of KISS ME, DEADLY, with his finger on the first italicized passage, where the girl puts Hammer's hand under her rain coat and he discovers she's naked. Hot-o-mighty! (as we used to say), talk about your Hot Stuff! (You can see what basically deprived lives we led in the 50s.)

John Black is the one who went on to discover THE REVOLT OF MAMIE STOVER and GOD'S LITTLE ACRE. He liked them as much, or more, than Spillane; but there was something about Spillane that's held my attention ever since. I've never been sure of just what it is, but maybe it's the conviction that he brings to his books, especially the Hammer books. You can almost feel Hammer's hate and violence in a way that Spillane's imitators never managed.

But they tried, and a lot of them were Spillane's friends. As Charlie Wells put it on the back of THE LAST KILL, "Yes, it was Mickey himself who showed me how to pack guts, gore, and hot, suspenseful action into a mystery yarn." Spillane wrote the blurb for the front cover of this 1955

9

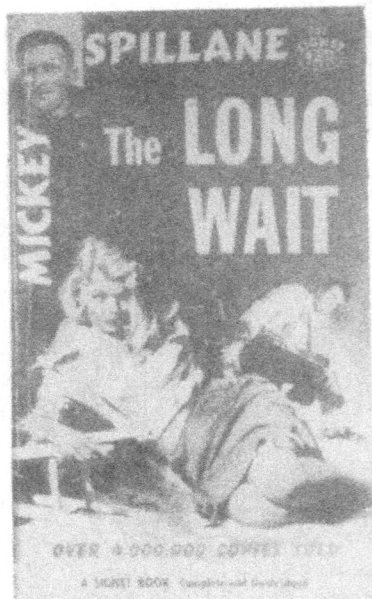

Signet editon. He also wrote cover (front and back) raves for Wells' 1954 Signet reprint, LET THE NIGHT CRY.

Spillane also let Gold Medal use his name on several books, including John D. MacDonald's THE DAMNED ("I wish I had written this book"-- Mickey Spillane) which was first printed in 1952, and on Peter Rabe's 1956 HOUSE IN NAPLES ("This guy is good" -- Mickey Spillane). Spillane's name doesn't appear on the two Gold Medal books by "Garrity," KISS OFF THE DEAD (1960) and CRY ME A KILLER (1961); but when this author wrote DRAGON HUNT as Dave J. Garrity (Signet, 1967), Spillane wrote the cover blurb ("Guts, action. . .the kind of stuff I like to read") and appeared in the back cover photo with the author. Garrity now writes as David J. Gerrity. Of his book THE NEVER CONTRACT (Signet, 1975), Spillane said on the the cover, "I wish I had written it!"

If publishers coundn't get Spillane to write jacket copy, they'd write it themselves, using his name, as is done on the back cover of Duane Yarnell's MANTRAP (Crest, 1957), "packs a wallop like Mickey Spillane." Or better yet, they would use a newspaper quotation which compared the writer to Spillane, as on the front cover of the 1956 Crest reprint of Donald Stokes' CAPTIVE IN THE NIGHT: ". . .will be fascinating to readers of Mickey Spillane," from the New York Herald Tribune. Or on the 1953 Signet reprint of Jimmy Shannon's THE DEVIL PASSKEY: "Written in the Mickey Spillane style," from the Birmingham News.

Despite all this passing around of his name, Spillane remained an original; and no matter how hard the imitators tried, no one was ever able to come up with exactly the right formula. No one could ever do it quite like the master.

And Spillane is a master. His writing may be fine, but it's effective. Consider the following from THE BIG KILL:

It was the only kind of talk they
knew. . . . I snapped the side of the rod
across his jaw and laid the flesh open to
the bone. He dropped the sap and staggered
into the big boy with a scream starting
to come out of his throat only to get it
cut off in the middle as I pounded his
teeth back into his mouth with the end of
the barrel. The big guy tried to shove
him out of the way. He hot so mad he
came right at me with his head down and
I took my own damn time about kicking him
in the face. He smashed into the door and
lay there bubbling. So I kicked him again
and he stopped bubbling.

It goes on in the same vein, but you get the idea.
That last sentence, though, is the classic, and it
makes Spillane what he is: tough, with no compro-
mise. There's nothing like the real thing.

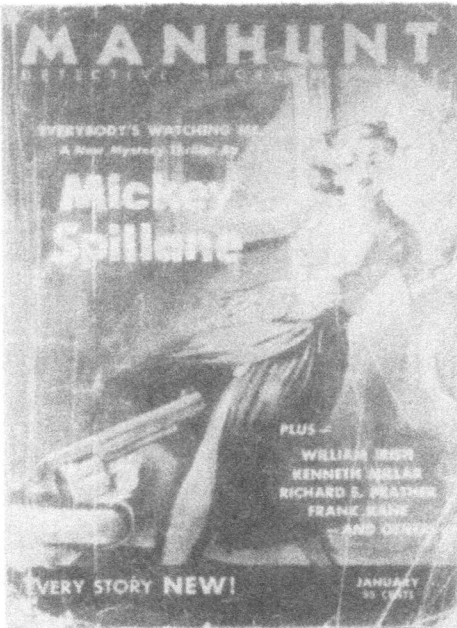

MANHUNT, vol 1,
Number 1 January
1953 featuring
"Everybody's
Watching Me" by
Mickey Spillane

TWO LONELY NIGHTS WITH MICKEY SPILLANE

ERCERPTS FROM AN INTERVIEW
BY MICHAEL S. BARSON

[The following interview with Mickey Spillane
was conducted over a two day period in March
1976 by Michael Barson at Spillane's home
in South Carolina. Michael eventually wrote
his Master's Thesis on Spillane and is cur-
rently working on his PhD in American Cul-
ture at Bowling Green State University.
Michael plans to write his dissertation on
the history and cultural impact of paperbacks
in America. The bulk of his lengthy interview will appear in TAD in the fall of 1979.
The complete interview tape is housed at
Bowling Green University audio center archives.
A great deal of the interview (not featured
here) concerns Spillane's musings on politics,
welfare, the CIA, the FBI, the Blacks, and
his wife.]

MS: *Yeah, you get into trends occasionally. Most
of the time I did something a little different. I
started a trend and then I fulfilled it. You start
your own trends going.*

MB: You said you can't write for today's market,
you have to write for tomorrow's market.

MS: *That's right. It's like surfboarding: You've
got to be in front of the wave, not the top. You
see, you ride ahead of the crest of the wave. You
set it up.*

MB: So what was this wave you started, the Mike
Hammer thing?

MS: *Yeah. I knew what people wanted. They didn't*

want wishy-washy heroes. When I started the Mike Hammer thing everybody was fresh out of the war. Guys were out there, they had seen violence, real violence is never going to bother anybody. And you've got a pretty horny bunch during the war, too. A little more sex in the story wasn't going to bother them, it was going to set them up for what was to come. So when I wrote I, THE JURY, I knew what was going to happen.

MB: That style of writing Mike's thoughts in italics when he's had this breakthrough...

MS: See, I always recognize the fact that reading is as much visual as it is mental. That's why all this stuff in here comes out in italics.
    When I read I, THE JURY now...This is a good story written back in an old style. I write so much differently now; when you read THE ERECTION SET you can see that.

MB: Well, I saw that in THE LAST COP OUT. It seems to be much more tightly plotted than--

MS: I haven't got anything that's dragged out. THE ERECTION SET is the longest book I've ever written. Everything is so damn tight that the editors can't cut anything. There's nothing to cut out of my books. I learned that a long time ago when I was doing comics. I don't write for pages. You write your story, keep it tight. If you know that little secret of writing tight you got a big advantage over a lot of other people.

MB: So, do you like a guy like Ernest Hemingway who tried to put as few words down as he could to get--

MS (Laughs): Oh, he used to hate my guts! This was so bad...I never met Hemingway and I never read a lot of Hemingway. But he wrote a story for

14

BLUEBOOK magazine and, boy, he just tore me apart.
Of how I was no good, this, that and the next thing.
So I'm on a television show and this guy said to
me, "Did you see that piece that Hemingway wrote
about you in BLUEBOOK?" And I said, "Hemingway
who?" So he gets wind of this thing and he blows
up. Oh, man, he wants to tear me apart.

Well, he didn't realize that I was working
in an editorial way for Signet. And he turned in
a book--a book?--a novelette, a little eight page
novelette, and he wanted $25,000 for it. The title
of the story was "The Old Man and the Sea." So
I told him to go screw himself and take it back.
He took it back and he writes the book about it,
which was very dull. You can't do a man and a
fish well forever throughout a book.

Anyway, there's a restaurant called the
Chesapeake down in the Upper Matacombe in Florida.
Behind the cash register this girl--I used to go
diving with this girl all the time--this girl's
got these pictures of celebrities. There's a
big picture of me, and there's a picture of
Hemingway right next to me. One day Hemingway comes
in and he sees it and he says, "You either take
mine down or you take his down." She looked at
him, went over and took his down and gave it to
him.

MB: Good old Papa!

MS: He could not stand success from other people
who did not care about success. If you wanted to
be a big one and act it...But you couldn't be just
a plain old shit-kicker type.

MB: Well, you guys were natural rivals in a way...

MS: There's so much room on the market for people,
you can't--don't get competitive. I can't imitate
myself, so don't let somebody else imitate me. It
was like when Richard Prather was coming out in the

early days with his character and it was a copy of Mike Hammer: a guy with white hair and all this kind of stuff. And he was working so hard imitating me that he wasn't doing the best job that he could've. Had he done his own line he would have been a better writer...

I don't know why writers are so notoriously sensitive, but they're worse than actors. If they get kicked in the head, you know, they don't want to write anymore.

MB: Are you talking about sales or reviews?

MS: *I'm just talking reviews. They can get big sales but...Look at the big sales I have and the lousy little reviews I got. I don't care. The only place I want my name is on a check anyway. That's why I'm in business. As long as I got lousy reviews, I got great sales.*

MB: I saw that THE LAST COP OUT had good reviews. On the back cover...Is this Sherry [Spillane's second wife] too?

MS: *Yeah, that's her, from the rear end.*

MB: I thought maybe it was, but I wasn't sure. Do you get into the packaging of these paperbacks at all?

MS: *Well, I'm a good photographer, and I shot all these things myself.* [Covers of THE ERECTION SET and THE LAST COP OUT].

MB: You shot these yourself? They're great!

MS: *The hard cover came out great on this because we used the leg to go up the spine. It was never done before. I won an award for that. I won an award for the best cover of the year, but I couldn't accept it because I wasn't an art director.*

16

MB: How did you promote this?

MS: *See, we did something different on book tour. I never go out and sit in a desk and sign autographs on hard cover books. We go to supermarkets, discount stores, 5 & 10's, drug stores, any place where a mass market meets, we do reprints.*

MB: Yeah, like the thirty I brought with me.

MS: *Sometimes we have thousands of people in these places that come the next day and wait and these people are buying books. Now this is the market that you make your money from. They give you information that you never get from the hard book class. I've had a lot people tell me, "Boy, when I finished that book I was crying." "Boy, that was great the way that happened." Very satisfied customers.*

****FANTASY NEWSLETTER****

THE BEST IS GETTING BETTER!!

FANTASY NEWSLETTER which features the most up to date information available on hardbacks, paperbacks, authors, publishers, conventions, etc. in the science fiction/fantasy genre is e-x-p-a-n-d-i-n-g to bring you the BEST coverage possible. The new look which begins with the January issue will feature art work by Stephen Fabian and nonfiction by Karl Edward Wagner and Fritz Leiber. Moreover, FN will feature interviews with and articles on authors, artists, and publishers in the science fiction/fantasy genre. To cover these many extras, FANTASY NEWSLETTER will expand to 32 pages per month and sport a slick cover.

Don't miss an issue; Write NOW to: Paul Allen, 1015 West 36th St., Loveland, CO. 80537. 12 issues for $12. Well worth the price!

17

THE PENGUIN STORY

[The following short history of British Penguin paperbacks was sent to PQ by Eric Tucker, Surrey, England. See "Letters" section.]

On 30 July 1935 bookshops, bookstalls and Woolworth counters first displayed ten new paper-backed books in bold orange, blue and green covers decorated with a black and white penguin. They were the fruit of several months hard work by Allen Lane, the young managing director of the Bodley Head. During these months he had discussed with many fellow publishers his idea to reprint in paper-back, good books at the price of a packet of ten cigarettes. The publishing world, still in the financial doldrums following the slump, said that it could not succeed. Undeterred, Allen Lane went ahead and printed the books.

The first ten Penguins, all priced at sixpence, were ARIEL by Andre Maurois, A FAREWELL TO ARMS by Ernest Hemingway, POET'S PUB by Eric Linklater, MADAME CLAIRE by Susan Ertz, THE UNPLEASANTNESS AT THE BELLONA CLUB by Dorothy Sayers, THE MURDER ON THE LINKS by Agatha Christie, TWENTY-FIVE by Beverley Nichols, WILLIAM by E.H. Young, GONE TO EARTH by Mary Webb and CARNIVAL by Compton Mackenzie.

To begin with Penguins were distributed by the Bodley Head. Penguin Books however, were not a Bodley Head undertaking and on 1 January 1936 a new company, Penguin Books Ltd, was formed with a capital of 100. The new company took over its own distri-bution and for a warehouse and packing room it rented the crypt of Holy Trinity Church, Euston Road in London. From this rather bizarre establishment Penguin Books operated for its first eighteen months. Towards the end of 1937 the whole firm moved out to Harmondsworth near Heathrow Airport, where it is still situated.

At the time of the move the Penguin list had reached well over one hundred titles and the policy of providing good books for every taste was being maintained with great success. A new series, Pelicans, had been launched. The First title was George Bernard Shaw's INTELLIGENT WOMAN'S GUIDE TO SOCIALISM, CAPITALISM, SOVIETISM AND FASCISM. Shaw wrote the sections on Sovietism and Fascism especially for the Pelican edition making it, as he pointed out, 'a Shaw first edition at sixpence'.

In the year of Mussolini's state visit to Hitler's Germany and the bombing of Guernica, Penguins reflected the deep public concern at the trend of political events, already moving fast towards war. The first Penguin Special, Edgar Mowrer's GERMANY PUTS THE CLOCK BACK, a sharp warning of Hitler's intentions in Europe, was published. Within two years it had been followed by nearly fifty further Specials on matters of importance and public interest including BLACKMAIL OR WAR?, THE AIR DEFENCE OF BRITAIN, THE JEWISH PROBLEM, WHAT HITLER WANTS, and THE PRESS.

The war years saw the continuing growth of the range of Penguins. King Penguins were started in 1939; a volume of Tennyson's poems was the first of the Penguin Poets and Puffin Story Books were launched with the publication of WORZEL GUMMIDGE which is still in print today.

Another product of the war years was the first Penguin Classic. During the many boring hours on firewatch in the blitz, Dr. E.V. Rieu had made a new translation of Homer's ODYSSEY, and this was published in January 1946. Later Rieu translated the ILIAD and both sold over one million copies.

The first Penguin colophon was designed by an office boy at the Bodley Head, Edward Young. In 1954 Commander Young's book ONE OF OUR SUBMARINES was published as Penguin 1000.

The list continued to grow over the years and most of the major writers of the century have been published in the Penguin lists. Gradually paper-backs became more and more acceptable and Penguin was always at the head of the boom in sales and

19

quality.

In 1960 Allen Lane decided to publish D.H. Lawrence's novel LADY CHATTERLEY'S LOVER in an unabridged edition. He was immediately prosecuted under the Obscene Publications Act. LADY CHATTERLEY'S LOVER was the first book to be tried under the act which allowed expert witnesses to be called to testify to the literary merit of a publication. Some of the major literary figures in Britain appeared on the Lady's behalf during her famous trial at the Old Bailey. The case was dismissed and the book became an immediate best-seller.

Penguin books became a public company in April 1961 with Allen Lane retaining the majority shareholding. The share issue was 160 times over subscribed.

Allen Lane, who had entered publishing at the age of 16 in 1919, was knighted in 1953. In 1969 he was made a Companion of Honour; he recieved many Honorary Doctorates and was Hon Fellow of Royal College of Art, Fellow of the American Academy of Arts and Sciences and recieved the Gold Albert Medal from the Royal Society of Arts also in 1969.

This was the year he retired from Penguins (although he retained an active interest in the Company until his death). His retirement on 23 April, exactly 50 years from the day he had started with the Bodley Head, was marked by the publication in Penguin of ULYSSES by James Joyce, a book Lane had been instrumental in publishing in this country.

Following the death of Sir Allen Lane on 7 July 1970, Penguins merged with Longman and in 1971 became a wholly-owned subsidiary of Pearson Longman Ltd.

The list today is some 4000 titles long - still retaining the mix of high quality fiction, non fiction and childrens books. The company sells over 44 million books a year, approximately half of which are sold overseas. There are subsidiary companies in The United States, Canada, Australia

and New Zealand and the name of Penguin is known
almost throughout the world.

ROBERT JONAS   855-6726
100 Remsen Street
Brooklyn, New York 11201

FULL COLOR ART ORIGINALS FOR SALE:
(PRICES RANGE FROM $100 TO $150--WRITE FOR DETAILS)

CHARLES ERSKINE SCOTT WOOD	HEAVENLY DISCOURSE
EDITH HAMILTON	THE GREEK WAY TO WESTERN CIVILIZATION
SIGMUND FREUD	PSYCHOPATHOLOGY OF EVERYDAY LIFE
DUNN & DOBZHANSKY	HEREDITY, RACE AND SOCIETY
SAUL K. PADOVER	JEFFERSON
RICHARDS & MOCK	AN INTRODUCTION TO MODERN ARCHITECTURE
WADE MILLER	DEADLY WEAPON
PAUL MCGUIRE	A FUNERAL IN EDEN
J.W.N. SULLIVAN	THE LIMITATIONS OF SCIENCE
ERSKINE CALDWELL	TROUBLE IN JULY
LUDWIG BEMELMANS	HOTEL SPLENDIDE
FRANK GRUBER	THE TALKING CLOCK
HENRY JAMES	DAISY MILLER
ELEAZAR LIPSKY	KISS OF DEATH
ROBERT NATHAN	PORTAIT OF JENNIE
ALFRED NORTH WHITEHEAD	SCIENCE AND THE MODERN WORLD
JOHN GEARSON	THE VELVET WELL
FRANK GRUBER	THE SILVER JACKASS
GRAHAM GREENE	THE MINISTRY OF FEAR
RACHEL CARSON	UNDER THE SEA WIND
MULLER	THE USES OF HISTORY
SUSAN LANGER	PHILOSOPHY IN A NEW KEY (Presentation Sketch)

SEE WHAT THE BOYS IN

THE BACKWOODS WILL HAVE

(AND TELL THEM I'M HAVING THE SAME)

-------BILL CRIDER

There's no doubt in my mind that it's all Erskine Caldwell's fault. TOBACCO ROAD, GOD'S LITTLE ACRE, JOURNEYMAN. What titles! What covers on the paperback editions! They always promised more that they delivered, but seduced us all. Their hugh sales spawned that wonderful phenomenon of the 50s, the backwoods novel.

Remember John Faulkner, from PQ vol 1,

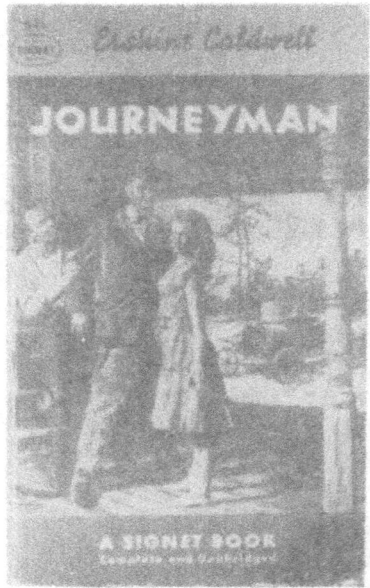

number 2? CABIN ROAD? THE SIN SHOUTER OF CABIN ROAD? Uncle Good and his lusty daughters? Faulkner had first titled his book SIDE ROAD. The publishers changed it, no doubt with Caldwell in mind. Compare the covers of CABIN ROAD and JOURNEYMAN. Notice the

ripe wenches just about to pop out of those tight
dresses. Notice the ramshackle cars, the cabins.
The word "backwoods" itself does not have to
appear, but if it can be used to effect, it should.
As indeed it does in such classics of the genre as
BACKWOODS TRAMP (GM, 1959) by Harry Whittington,
BACKWOODS HUSSY (Original Novels, 1952) and
BACKWOODS SHACK (Carnival Books, 1954 by Hallam

Whitney (Whittington, of course). There are also
elegant variations, as in William Fuller's BACK
COUNTRY (Dell, 1954) or Gail Jordan's BACK-COUNTRY
WENCH (Croydon, 1954). The latter was first published as RESTLESS WIFE, and you can see that it's
just not the same.
    If you couldn't work "back" into the title, a
variation of "cabin" was also acceptable, as in
SHACK ROAD (Original Novels, 1953) by Hallam
Whitney or SHANTY ROAD (Original Novels, 1954) by

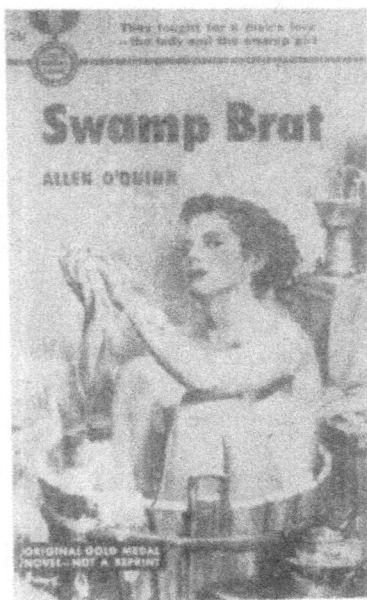

24

Whit Harrison (Whittington again). Also acceptable is the word "swamp" in place of "backwoods," as in Whit Harrison's SWAMP KILL (Phantom, 1951), Allen O'Quinn's SWAMP BRAT (GM, 1953) with its wonderful cover of the girl bathing in a wooden tub, Jack Woodford & John Thompson's SWAMP HOYDEN, and Robert Faherty's SWAMP BABE (Crest, 1960). The latter was originally called BIG OLD SUN, and again the difference is clear, especially as far as sales goes.

Still another variation calls for the word "girl" to appear in the title, along with some appropriately swampy scenery on the cover, or perhaps along with some

other backwoodsy words. fine examples may be found in many of the novels of Charles Williams (along with Harry Whittington another of the really expert practitioners of the paperback original). William's first book was HILL GIRL (GM, 1950), and he followed it with such classics as RIVER GIRL (GM Giant, 1951); BIG CITY GIRL (GM, 1951);

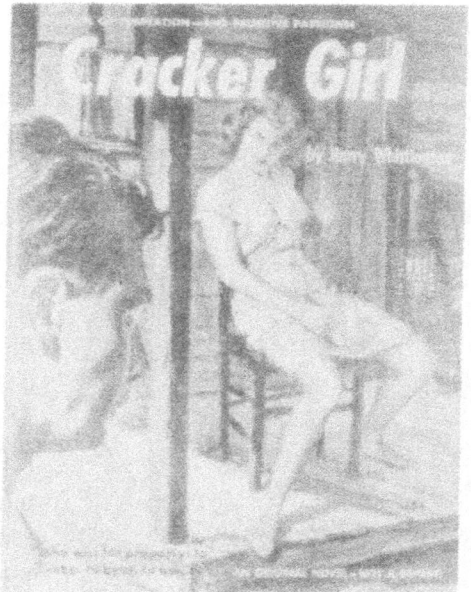

GIRL OUT BACK (Dell, 1958 -- and note that "Out Back"); and SCORPION REEF, a hardback which Dell cleverly re-titled GULF COAST GIRL for its paperback edition (no date). Then there're Harry Whittington's CRACKER GIRL (Universal, 1953) and Cord Wainer's MOUNTAIN GIRL (GM, 1952, 1960). (Cord Wainer is a really great pseudonym; the author's real name is Thomas Dewey, the creator of the famous Chicago detective, Mac). Variations on the "girl" theme would have to include Harry Whittington's A WOMAN ON THE PLACE (Ace, 1956) and Daniel White's SOUTHERN DAUGHTER (Avon, 1953).

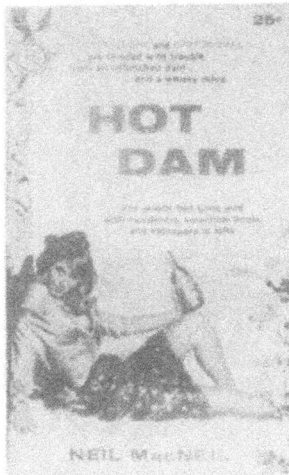

Not fitting into any of the title categories -- but just look at the covers-- are Whittington's ACROSS THAT RIVER (Ace, 1956), Neil MacNeil's HOT DAM, William

27

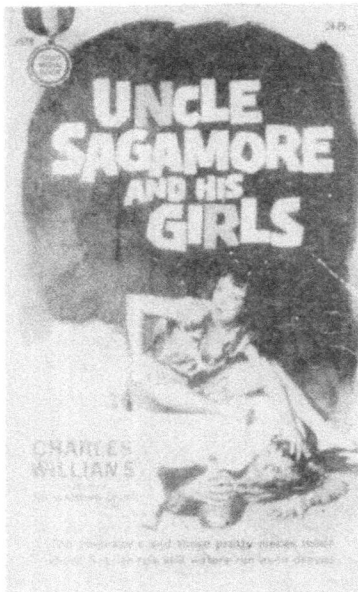

Fuller's GOAT ISLAND
(Dell, 1954), and Jim
Thompson's POP. 1280 (GM,
1964).

A double category
winner would be a book
with both "girls" and
"uncle" in the title.
Gold Medal writers win
with John Faulkner's
UNCLE GOOD'S GIRLS (1952,
1954) and Charles
Williams's UNCLE SAGAMORE
AND HIS GIRLS (1959).

Clearly the champion
writer of backwoods paperbacks is Harry Whittington.
The publisher with the
most titles is Gold Medal.
What made these books so
popular? That's a good
question. The promise of

28

sex? (look at those covers again). The indefin-
able lure of the backwoods, where men are men and
women are available? Your guess is as good as
mine. The appeal is there, that's for certain.
Even Kenneth Burke admitted that he enjoyed Erskine
Caldwell, though if memory serves he also compared
reading a Caldwell novel to playing with his toes.
Even THE NEW YORK TIMES BOOK REVIEW reviewed RIVER
GIRL (the second printing), though the reviewer
took time out to wonder why a writer with Williams's
talent was wasting his time on backwoods trash.
     Why did the backwoods genre tend to fade
away in the 60s? That's an easy one. It moved
(in its laundered versions) to TV, where it was
easier to watch than to read. Remember THE ANDY
GRIFFITH SHOW? THE BEVERLY HILBILLIES? GREEN
ACRES? THE REAL MCCOYS? If anything could kill
off a genre, GREEN ACRES could. But the books are
still out there, somewhere, waiting for you.

---

* * * BOOK SELLERS * * *

The following people sell paperbacks and some
hardbacks by mail. Most mail out book lists on a
regular basis and all are knowledgeable paperback
collectors.

BUNKER BOOKS (M.C. HILL)
P.O. Box 1638
Spring Valley, CA 92077
(714) 469-3296

HOWARD WATERHOUSE
P.O. Box 167
Upton, Mass. 01587
(617) 529-3703

STEVE LEWIS
62 Chestnut Rd.
Newington, CT 06111

BILL & PAT LYLES
77 High St.
Greenfield, MA 01301

JEFF MEYERSON
50 First Place
Brooklyn, NY 11231

If you sell paperbacks
via mail, we want to hear
from you.

S P O T L I G H T

"POCKETTES"

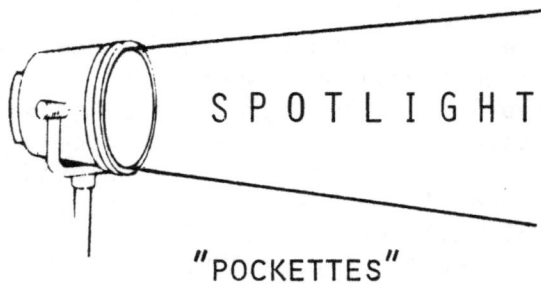

In 1972, Pocket Books introduced the descendents of Dell Dimers: Pockettes. But in twenty years the price had quintupled, and the younger version of the Dimers sold for 50¢. Pockettes were also about one third longer than the Dimers, running about 96 pages as opposed to 62-64 pages.

Despite the differences in price and length, Pockettes were based on the same ideas as ideas as Dell Dimers: short selections by well-known authors in an easy-to-carry format. Pockettes were advertised in the following manner:

> Pockettes, produced by Pocket Books
> for today's fast-paced society, is
> a collection of exciting mysteries,
> stirring romances and thrilling gothic
> adventures---all specially selected
> to provide a satisfying and pleasurable
> reading experience that can be enjoyed
> and completed in an afternoon or evening.
> Authored by world-famous, best-selling
> writers such as Faith Baldwin, Gertrude
> Schweitzer, Benjamin Siegel, Adela
> Rogers St. Johns, Jerome Weidman,
> Dorothy Eden, Vera Caspary, Frank Yerby,
> and many, many more, Pockettes will
> indeed bring you "the finest in reading
> at the lowest possible price."

Pockettes began with the number 50601. The first eight Pockettes are as follows:

50601   THE DOCTOR by Benjamin Siegel
50602   RUTH by Vera Caspary
50603   THE HOUSE BY THE SEA by Mignon Eberhart
50604   MISS ELIZABETH LANDON, M.D. by Gertrude
       Schweitzer
50605   A LINNET SINGING by Dorothy Eden
50607   THE DANGEROUS MRS. MALONE by Adela Rogers
       St. Johns
50608   "I, AND I ALONE" by Jerome Weidman
50609   MAGDA by Faith Baldwin

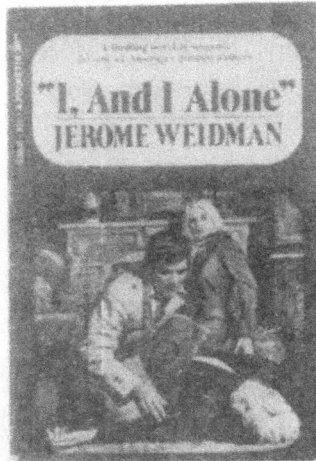

POCKETTE NUMBER 50608
(ACTUAL SIZE 3.9 x 5.8")

$ $ $ $ $ $ $ $ $

PQ now pays cash for your notes and articles---
see copyright page.

THE AMERICAN DETECTIVE SERIES

-----HOWARD WATERHOUSE
West Upton, Mass.

It was Reckless Ralph who got me started on this article...... Perhaps another time we could examine Reckless Ralph and his "Dime Novel Roundup" more extensively. For this article, however, Reckless Ralph Cummings provides the setting and background rather than occupying center stage.

I had heard of an older man who often went to the same yards sales as I, only one or two steps ahead. I finally met Ralph Cummings just one town away and found him with a mind full of 70 years of dealing with paper ephemera and a house full of that very same material. In general I shared the

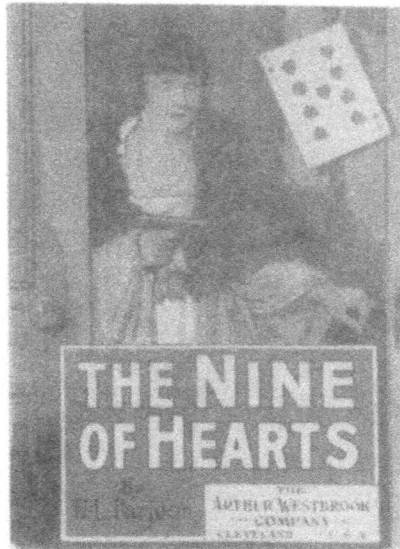

attitude many paperback collectors have against
the "pulp" of the early half of this century.
Ralph's Dime Novels and "Half-Dime Novels" then
were impressive but not really objects that fit
into my scope of collecting. Similarly, I was
not too impressed by the literary merit of the
"romantic" turn-of-the-century mind. Horatio
Alger and Nick Carter did appeal to a less sophis-
ticated and more unworldly period of time. Never-
theless as my acquaintance with Ralph grew (The
"Reckless" part comes from the title of the
Fanzine he edited for many years, "Reckless Ralph's
Dime Novel Round-up") I discovered a series published by Arthur Westbrook Company in Cleveland,
Ohio which deserves a niche in the incunabula file
of the true paperback book aficionado.

In the first place, the evidence in Ralph's
A case can be made that the "American Detective Series" brought out by Arthur Westbrook Company between 1906 and 1937 is a legitimate tran-
sitional stage (a literary "missing link") between
the Dime-Novel, pulp paper ephemera of pre WWI and
the slick, miniaturized mass-produced "modern"
paperback of the post WWII period. As such it is
worth our study, if only to learn once again that
no concept is a new as we like to think...

In the first place, the evidence in Ralph's
attic and elsewhere and the resources demonstrate
that "mass market" cheap paper editions were relatively as in abundance over one hundred years ago
as they are today. Bowker's HISTORY OF BOOK PUB-
LISHING IN THE UNITED STATES and Frank Schick's
PAPERBOUND BOOK IN AMERICA indicate that millions
of the early "paperbounds" were being published
at the time of the War Between the States.

> "Beadle & Co. had published over
> four million dime novels by 1865,
> the sales of individual titles
> ranged from 35,000 to 80,000..."
> Schick. PBIA p. 51

In the early days there was much pirating of
titles and authors and, much as we see today, the

THE
RED RAJAH
by
Capt Frederick Whittaker
THE
ARTHUR WESTBROOK
COMPANY
CLEVELAND   C.S.A.

success and failure of many publishers reflected
the economic condition of the nation.

By the turn of the century the "paperbounds"
were slumping and, in particular the Beadle firm
was in dissolution. The firm's assets went to M.
J. Ivers in New York City and then in 1905 when
Ivers went out of business the much traveled and
worn plates were sold to our central characters,
the Arthur Westbrook Company of "Cleveland - U.S.A."
as their logo succinctly puts it.

Westbrook published several series; an adventure series, a "love"series, but the one of great-
est interest to me was their American Detective
Series. In outline form I'll try to reinforce the
argument that this series fits our context:
Period: From 1906 to 1937 these titles were issued
and reissued with little or no internal evidence of

34

publication date or copyright or original source.
Size: The earlier books are about ¼ to ½ inch
greater in width and height than the later reprints;
the earlier being 5¼ by 7 inch, the later issues
being closer to 4 3/4th by 6 3/4th inch. All edges
are trimmed smoothly which is again more "modern"
that the rough pulps. Thus they were smaller than
a Murder Mystery Monthly, larger than a Dell and
about the same as a Collier paperback.
Cover Art: One of the most significant differences
between the 19th Century "paperbounds" and the 20th
Century "paperbacks" lies in the cover art. The
older books are usually sepia or monochromatic and
the art work is usually quite dated as to clothing
and posture. In the Westbrook covers we come to a
nearly "modern" art. They are disigned to catch
the eye with bright primary colors and the use of
shadow to make title letters stand out; and they
catch the mind's eye with "lurid" subjects, some
even quite suggestive for the period. One of my
favorites is the NINE OF HEARTS (B.L. Farjeon)
cover which combines an attractive female in de-
colletage with an automatic in her hand and a
vivid nine of hearts in the foreground. Not quite
the cast-iron bra school of the fifties but certainly more of an eye catcher than scenes of the
past.
Writers: The series did not develop as it was
first projected if we judge by the lists carried
on the rear cover. Early issues called for two
books by Doyle and two by Du Boisgoby which did
not appear. Since these titles were replaced by
"Old Sleuth" titles, it would seem that the problem
was copyright. However, the bulk of the list-
ultimately 59 titles carried authors of substance
(even if not with their permission?).

As can be seen from the check list, the list
started with Doyle and certainly these editions,
even if pirated are eminently collectible now.
But there are other writers of note. Fortune Du
Boisgoby is still read by followers of the early

period of detectival lore and Fergus Hume is
revered if not usually read. I happen to like
oddities in detective fiction and can find several
prototypes in the Westbrook offering- a woman
detective, a magician detective and a code or
cipher detective. Wonder if the creator of the
"Great Merlini" ever read "Mark Magic" when he was
a boy? Of course the series held many unappetiz-
ing titles, but then, what series doesn't?

Price and Distribution: As far as Reckless Ralph
and I can find out the Westbrook offerings had
full distribution throughout the Central and
Northeast states. He recalls buying them in New
York City and Buffalo and we have evidence of
Cleveland and Chicago. The rear cover mentions
the books were available through the mail for 20¢
each from the publisher and Ralph remembers paying
25¢ as well.

General Collectability: I submit that this would
be a fun series to collect. (Indeed, I'd like to
complete my own set which lacks the Doyles and a
few others.) They would make a good display of
an early 20th century cover art; they are relatively
limited in number (59 to the best of my knowledge);
and they fill an important historical gap.

```
1   SHERLOCK HOLMES................A. Conan Doyle
2   THE RED RAJAH..................Capt. Frederick
        Whittaker (Should have been STUDY IN SCARLET
        by A. Conan Doyle)
3   BEYOND THE CITY................A. Conan Doyle
4   A CASE OF INDENTITY............A. Conan Doyle
5   A SCANDAL IN BOHEMIA...........A. Conan Doyle
6   THE RED HEADED LEAGUE..........A. Conan Doyle
7   THE SIGN OF THE FOUR...........A. Conan Doyle
8   THE GIANT DETECTIVE IN FRANCE..Old Sleuth
        (Should have been THE WHITE COMPANY by
        A. Conan Doyle)
9   THE SURGEON OF GASTER FELL.....A. Conan Doyle
10  MILL STREET MYSTERY............Adeline Sargeant
11  THE BAG OF DIAMONDS............G. Manville Fenn
```

-- OVERSIGHT --

In the Summer 1979 issue, PQ failed to give
proper credit to Mark Schaffer's A Glance at Paperback
History. Schaffer's overview of paperback cover art
was originally printed in UTOPIA-10, a Dutch magazine,
each issue of which is devoted to a different topic.
UTOPIA-10 featured American paperback cover art.
PQ featured a review of UTOPIA-10 in the Winter 1978
issue.

PAPERBACK PROMOTIONALS

There have been quite a few changes in the
paperback book industry since LOST HORIZON first
showed its face. One area experiencing major
changes is paperback distribution. There was a
time when most publishers furnished their own
paperback racks to each retail store for their
own books. In fact, some agreements between
publisher/distributor/retail outlet provided that
only Pocket Books were to be placed in Pocket
Books' racks, only Bantam paperbacks in Bantam
racks, etc.

On the back
of the rack pictured
to the left, is
printed: "PROPERTY
OF POCKET BOOKS INC.
TO BE USED FOR
GENUINE POCKET
BOOKS ONLY." Today,
of course, publish-
ers and titles are
mixed all on one
rack and the racks
belong (in most
cases) to the
distributor.

As newer racks
were made, the older
ones were thrown in
the trash bin.
Fortunately the one
pictured survived
and except for a
few scars, it's in
good shape. This
rack holds approx-
imately 4 books per
slot and has 30

facings. It is 22½'' wide and stands 52½'' from the floor. It is extremely light weight and folds out at the back for easy set up. Like many of the racks today, it is made of wire -- but wire which is almost twice as thick as the wire used today. And unlike most of the new wire racks I find today, there is no wire ''bar'' in front of the first book to hold each slot of books in place. I have found this inch high wire on the new racks prevents causal browsing of the books at the back. Distributors today would do well to take a good look at their now forgotten racks in order to improve their new ones.

DEVOTEES OF DETECTION DROOL

OVER CRIME COLLECTOR'S CACHE

Allen J. Hubin, author of BIBLIOGRAPHY OF CRIME FICTION, founder--editor of THE ARMCHAIR DETECTIVE, editor of seven anthologies, and crime-fiction reviewer for the New York TIMES, is selling his collection of 25,000 different books en bloc. The collection includes 2,500 paperbacks of mystery, detection and suspense, many of them paperback originals. All books are reported in good condition, and with their purchase comes Hubin's 3x5 card file, giving not only author, title, publisher, date and edition but in most cases the first line of the story. If any of you collectors can cough up $155,000 for this collection, contact International Bookfinders, Inc., Box 1, Pacific Palisades, CA 90272.

INTERNATIONAL
YOU NAME IT, WE FIND IT.
BOOKFINDERS INC.

NOTES AND QUERIES

THE PAPERBACK REVIEW

Can anyone fill me in on the nature and fate
of THE PAPERBACK REVIEW? It was announced in the
July 18, 1960 issue of PUBLISHERS WEEKLY and
described as follows:

"THE PAPERBACK REVIEW, a 32-page rotagravure
newspaper supplement entirely devoted to paperback books, will make its first appearance in
October of this year. The supplement is the
brain child of Alan C. Gillespie of Book Report
Services, Inc., 101 Fifth Ave., N.Y. 3. Me
Gillespie in the past few months has been busy
signing up subscribers for PAPER REVIEW among
college bookstores, college newspapers, and
paperback bookstores in general. He recently
stated to PW that he had a subscription list
of 999,700. This figure includes, in addition
to the college papers and the bookstores, use
of several thousand copies of the supplement
by the VILLAGER, a Greenwich Village publication,
and by the Boston HERALD-TRAVELER, which plans
to run Mr. Gillespie's paper as its form of
special paperback issue. Mr. Gillespie is also
negotiating with other city newspapers for
the same use of the PR in place of a staff-
edited paperback supplement. The PR's second
edition is scheduled for February 1961. The
subscription arrangements with bookstores in-
volve the use of bookstore imprints on the front
and back covers of the supplement. A third
edition of the supplement is planned for
exclusive mailing to college professors. There
are also plans, still uncompleted, for a separat-
ed edition for high school teachers. Mr
Gillespie has reported to PW that among the
many college papers that will be carrying the
PR will be those at Harvard, Yale, Princeton,
University of Wisconsin, New York University,
Amherst, University of Chicago, Dartmough,

Middlebury, Oberlin, Penn State, Purdue, Reed, Smith, Swarthmore, Vassar and Wellesley. He also states that Kroch's & Brentano's in Chicago will be using the supplement in its paperback department.

The contents of the PAPERBACK REVIEW will consist of many listing of paperback books published in recent months, descriptive comments on paperbacks in specific fields of interest, and articles on various aspects of the paperback field. Mr. Gillespie expects to use in his first issue brief descriptions of paperbacks approved by Brooks Atkinson in the drama field, by Margaret Mead in anthropology and archeology, by Richard Morris in American history, by Mark Van Doren in poetry, and by other specialists."

Did THE PAPERBACK REVIEW ever venture away from purely academic paperbacks into the world of more collectable paperbacks, such as mysteries, science fiction, and westerns? How many issues of THE PAPERBACK REVIEW were published? Does anyone have a set? Why was it unsuccessful?

----Charlotte Laughlin

SUPERIOR REPRINTS

I can answer several of the questions about SUPERIOR REPRINTS asked by Charlotte Laughlin in "Help!" The Military Service Publishing Company (division of Stackpole Sons) began publishing SUPERIOR REPRINTS in November 1944. These paperbacks were in mass market format and sold for 25¢ each. They were bound with high quality paper, which featured a glossy finish on inside as well as outside covers. The front inside covers carried blurbs about the books, and the back covers carried advertisements for other SUPERIOR REPRINT paperbacks and/or a photograph featured on the books was the announcement, "ALL SUPERIOR REPRINTS ARE COMPLETE AND UNABRIDGED."

43

The Military Service Publishing Company continued publication of Superior Reprints through September 1945. In all, twenty-one titles were issued.
Military Service Publishing Company books, including
Superior Reprints, were distributed by Penguin.
When Ian Ballantine left Penguin for Bantam Books in
the fall of 1945, he took the Superior Reprints ac-
count with him. Through him, Bantam Books later
acquired the stock and rights to titles of Superior
Reprints. Seven or Eight Superior Reprints reappear
as Bantam 144-146, 148-151. (Bantam 147, ONLY THE
GOOD by Mary Collins, was never published by Superior Reprints.) In later Bantam paperbacks, such as
152 and 205, all twenty-one Superior Reprints are
advertised as available from Bantam. At least one
Superior Reprint title, M655, THE MIGHTY BLOCKHEAD
by Frank Gruber, was encased in a dustcover of the
usual Bantam format which bore the Bantam number 144
on the spine.

Following is a list of all twenty-one Superior
Reprint titles with their Superior Reprints numbers
at the left and with their publication dates at the

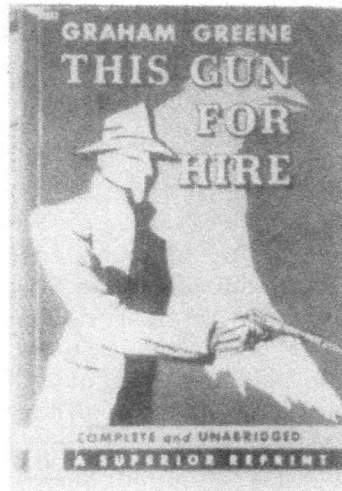

right, when known. Where appropriate the Bantam
numbers under which the books were reissued are
also given at the right.

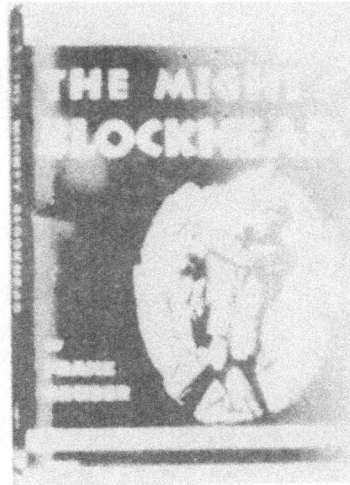

M637   WHITE MAGIC by Faith Baldwin; November 1944
M638   OL' MAN ADAM AND HIS CHILLUN by Roark
            Bradford
M639   UNEXPECTED NIGHT by Elizabeth Daly
M640   AN APRIL AFTERNOON by Philip Wylie
M641   FAMILY AFFAIR by Ione Sandberg Shriber;
            December 1944
M642   THE RYNOX MURDER MYSTERY by Philip MacDonald;
            December 1944, second printing January
            1945, third printing March 1945, later
            Bantam 146
M643   CARTOONS BY GEORGE PRICE
M644   EMBARRASSMENT OF RICHES by Marjorie Fischer
M645   MURDER IN MINK by Robert George Dean
M646   THE LOVE NEST AND OTHER STORIES by Ring
            Lardner; later Bantam 145
M647   INQUEST by Percival Wilde; March 1945
M648   ONE FOOT IN HEAVEN by Martzell Spence;
            March 1945

M649   THE NAVY COLT by Frank Gruber; April 1945,
           later Bantam 151
M650   THE INFORMER by Liam O-Flaherty; later
           Bantam 150
M651   MR. ANGEL COMES ABOARD by Charles B. Booth;
           May 1945
M652   THIS GUN FOR HIRE by Graham Greene; June 1945
M653   THE HOUSE WITHOUT THE DOOR by Elizabeth Daly
M654   ON ICE by Robert George Dean; August 1945,
           later Bantam 148
M655   THE MIGHTY BLOCKHEAD by Frank Gruber; September 1945, later Bantam 144
M656   A SAKI SAMPLER by Saki (H.H Munro); September 1945. Is this the same book by Saki, under the title THE SHE WOLF, published as Bantam 143?
M657   GOOD NIGHT, SHERIFF by Harrison Steeves; September 1945, later Bantam 149

I'm interested in buying Superior Reprints for which I lack the publication dates. (Obviously those are the ones I don't own.) I would also like to hear from anyone who has determined whether or not Superior Reprints' A SAKI SAMPLER and Bantam's THE SHE WOLF are the same book under different titles.

----James Tinsman

47

FLAGSHIP

In response to "Help!" on page 56 of the June 1979 PQ, I can offer this information. Flagship was a division (an imprint?) of Caravelle Books at 350 Lexington Avenue, New York, New York, 10016. Here are some of the titles:

THE EARLY DAYS OF AUGUST by J. R. Kovalsky
VALLEY OF THE MOON GODDESS by J. Thomas Hornsby
THE PLOT by K. P. Kelley
A MAN CALLED BLACK by Will Manson
THE RUNNER IS RED by J. R. Kovalsky
HOW TO CONTROL ARTHRITIS by Giraud W. Campbell
THE MATHEMATICIAN by Will Manson
BRAVO 9 by Will B. Day
A DEADLY GAME by Will Manson
THERAPUTIC SELF-HPYNOSIS by William C. Gibson
THE CHINESE CONUNDRUM by Will Manson
THE MAN FROM M.O.D. by Will B. Day
THE DANGEROUS ONE by Will Manson
MURDER...IN FULL VIEW by J.d. Forbes

Query: Who knows other titles or other pertinent information about Flagship Books?

----Jim Sanderson

ZEBRA STINKS!

Monarch Books may have been perfumed at one time, but Zebra Books stinks! At least that's my impression of the Zebra Books' personnel with whom I have had dealings while trying to write an article about Zebra for the volume, MASS MARKET PAPERBACK PUBLISHERS, which Bill Crider is editing for the ENCYCLOPEDIA OF AMERICAN PUBLISHERS. It will be published by Bruccoli/Clark Books in conjunction with Gale Research Company. From the reactions of the personnel at Zebra Books, you would think that Bruccoli/Clark Books and Gale Research Company were highly disreputable organizations and that Bill Crider and I were ax-murderers at the very least.

In searching through PUBLISHERS WEEKLY, I found several announcements of the publication of Grove Press Zebra books from 1969 to 1974. In the spring of 1974, two books (CHINA NIGHTS by Ralph Shaw and ZONE THEARPY by Vladimir Tuckak and Anika Bergon) were announced for summer publication by Zebra Books. However, these books were not published by Zebra but by Pinnacle Books. Finally, early in 1975, PUBLISHERS WEEKLY ANNOUNCED that Zebra Books was leading off its "independent line" with an autobiography of Marc Stevens, a star in porno films, who was described as "best known for his proportions." The book was appropriately titled 10½! My interest in porno film stars is limited, but I am interested in knowing the relationships between Zebra Books, Grove Press, and Pinnacle Books.

Consequently, early in June, I wrote two letters asking these and other intelligent questions to Walter Zacharius, chairman of the board of Zebra Books, and Leslie Gelbman, publicity director of Zebra Books. I enclosed a self-addressed, stamped envelope in each letter; but neither Mr. Zacharius nor Ms. Gelbman answered my letters. What they did with my stamps I don't know!

After waiting six weeks for a reply, I

decided to telephone Ms. Gelbman. The receptionist at Zebra Books left me on hold while she talked with Ms. Gelbman, only to return and tell me that Ms. Gelbman said that I should call back in an hour and talk to Roberta Grossman, president of Zebra Books. I called back in an hour and was told that President Grossman was still out to lunch and to call back in another hour. (It seemed odd to me that she was at lunch from before 1:30 till after 3:30, but I have since decided that President Grossman may be permanently out to lunch.)

I dutifully called back in another hour. Ms. Grossman was in this time, but she preferred that Ms. Gelbman speak with me. Ms. Gelbman had been in the office the first time I called, and if she had talked to me then, she could have saved me the expense of two more long-distance calls; but such considerations are nothing to these big-time publishing executives! No sooner had I asked my questions about Zebra's 1974 relationship to Pinnacle Books and earlier connection with Grove Press Books than Ms. Gelbman had to run ask Pres. Grossman the answer; but Madame President would not talk with me directly. Ms. Gelbman explained that she couldn't answer my questions herself because she hadn't been with the company from the years 1969 to 1974. (Since the company did not begin operations until 1975, I had already assumed that she had not been with the company prior to that time!) After leaving me on hold again, Ms. Gelbman returned to say that since my questions involved "corporate matters" President Grossman couldn't answer them over the telephone and that if I would send her my article in its present state she would be happy to reply. Mustering what reserves of courtesy I had left, I explained that since I had already written to her personally and to Mr. Zacharius and received no reply, I placed no faith in their replying to a letter this time. So after two letters (including SASE's) and three telephone calls, the personnel at Zebra Books has still refused to answer my questions. Now that stinks!

As a matter of review, I hope that Zebra Mystery Puzzlers fail as miserably as they so richly deserve to do. I read a few of them for the article I'm doing; and I can assure you that they are as stupid as the personnel at Zebra is rude. For example, the first Zebra Mystery Puzzler, YOU'LL DIE WHEN YOU HEAR THIS by Marjorie J. Grove, is about an exhibitionist gossip columnist who lets other people get killed in order to advance her own career by finding out the identity of the killer. This is the heroine, not the villain!) The book is full of old jokes and every cliche imaginable. The heroine is said to have breasts which are small "but young and ripely firm." On the next page she is described dressing: "She dressed quickly, choosing bikini panties and an uplift bra that did wonders for her bosom." Now, who cares what kind of panties she wore; and if her breasts are so "young and ripely firm" why does she need an uplift bra to do wonders for her bosom?   `

In addition to this sort of stupidity, the book is an unashamed name-dropper, evidently trying to impress the poor little reader with the names of Hollywood shops and res- taurants. The book also has an obsession with food: it describes in detail everything the dubious heroine eats. To make matters worse, the reader is told that on a certain busy morning the heroine did not have time to eat breakfast; but then an entire paragraph is used to tell what she would have eaten if she had had time! Needless to say, what she would have eaten if she

had had time (which she did not) included a handful of French terms as well as the brand name of the preserves she would have eaten if the poor dear had only had time.

The list of literary atrocities could go on, but I must give some attention to artistic atrocities. The interior illustrations (which are supposed to give clues to the identity of the murderer) are the most crudely executed drawings I've ever seen in a professionally produced book.

If I had had time to eat breakfast this morning (which I did not), I believe that I would have had roast Zebra. Even a mystery puzzler's attempts to impress readers with exotic foods can't top that one!

> [I've recently heard from Walter J. Hibbert, Jr., in response to "Help!". He says that Zebra was founded by person(s) associated with Lancer Books (Mr. Zacharius, who didn't answer my letter, no doubt), that went bankrupt. Grove Press, Pinnacle, Lancer, Zebra: Now that's a puzzler!]

----Charlotte Laughlin

COLLECTING PAPERBACKS?

CP? is a bi-monthly newsletter on paperback collecting. CP? features checklists and comments on paperbacks of all genres from 1938 to the present. Each 8½" x 11" issue provides fascinating reading on every page. Numerous paperback reproductions compliment almost every article. This publication is a must for the serious paperback collector. For details write to: LANCE CASEBEER, 934 S.E. 15th Street, Portland, OR 97214.

HARRY WHITTINGTON -- STILL A WINNER

As readers of PQ from the beginning (Volume I, Number 1) know, Harry Whittington has been writing paperback originals for almost thirty years. Unfortunately, despite praise from Anthony Boucher in THE NEW YORK TIMES BOOK REVIEW and in SATURDAY REVIEW, Whittington's work has never really received its critical due. The first PQ interview and Bill Crider's first "Paperback Writers" column were our modest attempt to remedy that situation. While we can't claim credit, we can at least be glad that others are now catching on. WEST COAST REVIEW OF BOOKS is one of the few slick publications which give much attention to paperback originals, but each year for the past three WCRB has been giving its "Porgie" awards to the best originals of the year. This year Harry Whittington won two, the third prize in the "contemporary" category for RAMPAGE (Gold Medal) under his own name, and the

second prize in the "fiction based on fact"
category for PANAMA (Gold Medal) under his Ashley
Carter pen-name. (Judy Crider reviewed PANAMA in
an earlier issue of PQ.) It's been a long time
coming, but maybe at last Harry Whittington's work
will recieve the recognition it deserves.

WATERHOUSE BOOKS
BOX 167
WEST UPTON, MASS. 01587
(617) 529-3703

WILL PUBLISH FOUR LISTS AS FOLLOWS:

OCT. '79 HARDCOVER MYSTERIES (BETTER GRADE)

NOV. '79 DELL MAPBACKS

JAN. '80 HARDCOVER MYSTERY BARGAINS

FEB. '80 POCKET BOOKS, AVONS, POPULAR
LIBRARY & RARE ITEMS.

EACH LIST IS ABOUT TEN PAGES WITH NOTES AND COMMENT--
SEND $1.00 FOR ONE LIST OR $2.00 FOR ALL FOUR LISTS.
☆ ☆ ☆ ☆ ☆
CURRENT WANTS: MURDER MYSTERY MONTHLY #47, THE
BLOND, THE GANGSTER AND THE PRIVATE EYE.
YOGI BOOKS: STUART TOWNE, DEATH
FROM NOWHERE.
POPULAR LIBRARY: Hugh Wiley, MURDER
BY THE DOZEN.
FANTASY & SCIENCE FICTION MAGAZINE/
DIGEST: VOL 1, #3 & #6; VOL 2, #2-6; VOL 3,
#1,#5, & #6.
LION/RED CIRCLE: #1,2,4,7,12 (LION
FROM HERE ON) #30,76,78,83,98,103,113,119,125,
129,133,135,136,137,160,162,166,168,169,172,175,
178,179,183,190,194,195,196,202,208,221,231,& up.

BUNKER BOOKS
M.C. HILL
P.O. BOX 1638
SPRING VALLEY, CA.
92077

(714) 469-3296

WANT TO BUY OR TRADE FOR:

DELL GREAT MYSTERY LIBRARY: D217, D227, D255, D275, D332, D343, D356, D323, D376.

GREEN DOOR MYSTERY: R917, R919, R931, R1066, R1123, R1269, R1292, X1682, X1514.

SAINT MYSTERY LIBRARY:
    118   STAIRWAY TO MURDER
    119   WITNESS TO DEATH
    120   MURDER SET TO MUSIC
    121   THE FRIGHTENED MILLIONAIRE
    122   MURDER MAID IN MOSCOW
    123   MURDER IN THE FAMILY
    124   DEATH STOPS AT A TOURIST CAMP
    125   RED SNOW IN DARJEELING
    126   EXECUTIONER'S SIGNATURE
    127   MURDER SEEKS AN AGENT
    128   LET HER KILL HERSELF
    129   INNOCENT BYSTANDER
    130   DEATH WALKS IN MARBLE HALLS

RED ARROW BOOKS:
    1   CHRISTIE, A.   THIRTEEN AT DINNER
    2   JONES, J.   MURDER ON HUDSON
    3   RHODE, J.   MURDERS ON PRAED STREET
    4   KETCHUM, P.   DEATH IN THE LIBRARY
    5   POPKIN, Z.   DEATH WEARS A WHITE GARDENIA
    6   MUSPRAT, E.   MY SOUTH SEA ISLAND
    7   RIIS, S.M.   YANKEE KOMISAR
    8   SMITH, L.D.   GIRL HUNT

BUNKER BOOKS(cont.)

9	BEEDING, F.	THE SEVEN SLEEPERS
10	MASON, F.V.W.	CAPTAIN NEMISIS
11	MOORE, O.	WINDSWEPT
12	WILLIAMS, B.A.	PIRATES PURCHASE

REX STOUT MYSTERY MAGAZINE (Digest Size)
NERO WOLFE MYSTERY MAGAZINE (Digest Size)

-- THE AGE OF THE UNICORN --

EVERY READER OF PQ should find something to
like about THE UNICORN. The October 1979 issue
features an article on the top 25 Shadow novels,
with opinions from numerous experts, including Will
Murray (who put the article together), Robert Weinberg,
Frank Hamilton, and others. There's also an index
to DR. YEN SIN, along with a discussion of the work
of Dennis Lynds by John Edwards and an article on
the mystery novels of Edgar Box (better known, pro-
bably, as Gore Vidal) by George Kelley. And more.
The ads and want lists are especially interesting.
THE UNICORN is available from Cook & McDowell
Publications, 3318 Wimberg Avenue, Evansville,
Indiana 47712. Subscriptions are $6.00 for six
issues, bulk mail or $12.00 first class. Artwork
and reproductions are first rate.

Mike Cook, editor of THE UNICORN, is also pre-
paring the first semi-pro mystery fiction magazine
that we at PQ are aware of. It will be called
SKULLDUGGERY, and the first issue will feature
stories by Bill Pronzini and Barry Malzberg, Michael
Avallone, and Mark Mansell. Subs are available from
the above address for $8.00 per year (the magazine
will be a quarterly), and all issues will be mailed
first class. If the quality is up there in a league
with THE UNICORN, every mystery fan will want to
subscribe immediately.

www.ingramcontent.com/pod-product-compliance
Lightning Source LLC
Chambersburg PA
CBHW021225020426
42331CB00003B/475